National Park Explorers

YELLOWSTONE

by Sara Gilbert

CREATIVE EDUCATION · CREATIVE PAPERBACKS

TABLE OF CONTENTS

A bison grazes in Yellowstone.

WELCOME TO YELLOWSTONE NATIONAL PARK!

What a tall arch! Look at the snowy mountains.
You might see a bear or an elk on the road. You   5
are in a wild place!

Yellowstone is the oldest national park in the United States. It became a park in 1872. It is in Wyoming. You will see mountains, forests, lakes, and streams there.

★ Yellowstone National Park
■ Wyoming

6

A snow-covered mountain (above); Lower Yellowstone Falls (right)

HOT WATER

Yellowstone has geysers and hot springs. The springs are pools of water. They are heated by the earth. There are more than 300 geysers in the 3,472-square-mile (8,992 sq km) park.

Old Faithful is a popular geyser. It shoots hot water high into the air. It does this every 35 to 120 minutes throughout the day.

Fishing Cone geyser (above); Old Faithful (right)

WILD IN
THE WEST

Yellowstone has more than 200 kinds of wild animals. Grizzly bears, wolves, and elk live there. **Bison** have lived in Yellowstone for hundreds of years.

More than a thousand wildflowers are **native** to the park. There are many kinds of pine trees, too.

A moose calf and mother (below); pine trees (right)

TAKE A HIKE

Three million people visit Yellowstone each year.
Many go between May and September.

You can hike on trails. Or you can fish in the lakes and rivers. You can also ride horses or camp.

A boardwalk and steam (above); camping near Colter Peak (right)

Always look out for animals. Do not get too close to them. **Rangers** tell hikers to make noise. Yell, "Hey, Bear!" as you are walking!

Coyotes, bears, and visitors enjoy the park's forests.

Activity

CREATE A MODEL GEYSER

Materials needed:
Baking soda
Plastic soda or juice
  bottle, with lid
Needle or other small,
  pointy object
Warm water

Step 1: Find an adult to help you. Use the needle or sharp object to make a hole in the lid of the bottle.

Step 2: Fill the plastic bottle about three-quarters full of warm water. Then add a spoonful of baking soda.

Step 3: Quickly replace the lid, holding your finger over the hole.

Step 4: Shake the bottle a few times. What will happen when you remove your finger from the hole?

Glossary

bison — large, hairy animals native to North America and Europe

geysers — springs that occasionally shoot hot water into the air

native — original to a certain place

rangers — people who take care of a park

Read More

McHugh, Erin. *National Parks: A Kid's Guide to America's Parks, Monuments, and Landmarks*. New York: Black Dog & Leventhal, 2012.

Petersen, David. *Yellowstone National Park*. Danbury, Conn.: Children's Press, 2001.

Websites

Kids Discover: National Parks
http://www.kidsdiscover.com/spotlight/national-parks-for-kids/
See pictures from the parks and learn more about their history.

WebRangers
http://www.nps.gov/webrangers/
Visit the National Park Service's site for kids to find fun activities.

Index

Published by Creative Education and Creative Paperbacks
P.O. Box 227, Mankato, Minnesota 56002 • Creative Education
and Creative Paperbacks are imprints of The Creative Company
www.thecreativecompany.us

Design and production by Christine Vanderbeek
Art direction by Rita Marshall
Printed in the United States of America

Photographs by Alamy (SuperStock), Corbis (Ingo Arndt/Minden
Pictures, Peter Barritt/Robert Harding World Imagery, Tim Fitzhar-
ris/Minden Pictures, Robbie George/National Geographic Creative,
Bryan Mullennix/Tetra Images, Tom Murphy/National Geographic
Creative, Pat O'Hara, Eleanor Scriven/Robert Harding World
Imagery), Dreamstime (Wisconsinart), Getty Images (Kick Images),
Shutterstock (Tarchyshnik Andrei, Sascha Burkard, Colin Edwards
Wildside, BW Folsom, Ruslan Grechka, hdsidesign, Eric Isselee,
Paul Knowles, Mayskyphoto, PFlynnPhoto, Rambleon, Schalke
fotografie/Melissa Schalke, Mark Smith, winnond)

Library of Congress Cataloging-in-Publication Data
Gilbert, Sara. • Yellowstone / by Sara Gilbert. • p. cm. —
(National park explorers) • *Summary*: A young explorer's introduc-
tion to Wyoming's Yellowstone National Park, covering its geyser-
filled landscape, plants, animals such as bison, and activities such as
camping and fishing. • Includes index. • ISBN 978-1-60818-634-1
(hardcover) • ISBN 978-1-62832-242-2 (pbk) • ISBN 978-1-56660-
671-4 (eBook) • 1. Yellowstone National Park—Juvenile literature.
I. Title.

F722.G47 2016
978.7'52—dc23 2014048724

CCSS: RI.1.1, 2, 3, 4, 5, 6, 7, 10; RI.2.1, 2, 3, 5, 6, 7; RI.3.1, 3, 5, 7;
RF.1.1, 3, 4; RF.2.4

HC 9 8 7 6 5 4 3
First Edition PBK 9 8 7 6 5 4 3 2 1